Original title:
Spaghettification Sonnets

Copyright © 2025 Creative Arts Management OÜ
All rights reserved.

Author: Atticus Thornton
ISBN HARDBACK: 978-1-80567-836-6
ISBN PAPERBACK: 978-1-80567-957-8

A Convection of Cosmic Essences

In the kitchen of space, where the stars twirl,
Noodles collide with a cosmic swirl.
Galactic chefs mix up sugar and spice,
Pouring stardust over pasta, oh so nice.

Gravity's a prankster, pulling things tight,
Turning angel hair into a strange fright.
To measure a portion, just grab a black hole,
And hope your dinner's not out of control.

Celestial Dishes of Time

Planets are plates in a dinner divine,
Served with a side of celestial wine.
Quantum forks twirl in a twinkling haze,
While timelines bounce like a spaghetti craze.

The sauce is a swirl of history's blend,
Each tomato's a tale that will never end.
Whisking through eras, we taste the delight,
Of meals made in moments that dance out of sight.

Fettuccine Dreams in the Otherworld

In dreams made of fettuccine and cream,
We savor the flavors that pop and beam.
Butterfly noodles fly through darker skies,
Twisting through realms, to our great surprise.

Eldritch flavors from realms beyond reach,
Tickling our tongues like a cosmic speech.
As laughter erupts at each tangled bite,
Our forks are the comets that zoom through the night.

Stars and Sauce in the Cosmos

Twinkling stars drop in the pot with a splash,
Mixing up wonder with an interstellar dash.
A supernova simmers, bubbling with cheer,
While milky comets dance, oh so near.

With every big bang, new recipes rise,
Galaxies stir in a pasta surprise.
Grab a plate of the universe's delight,
And savor the chaos in the velvety night.

Infinite Twists of Existence

In the cosmic kitchen, a chef spins,
Pasta twists dancing, a chorus of grins.
Reality noodles, stretching so wide,
Gravity's sauce in which we all slide.

Galaxies boil in a pot of delight,
Strands of confusion twirl, what a sight!
With forks like rockets, we launch our dreams,
In this wacky universe, nothing's as it seems.

Chaotic Noodle Fantasies

Once I tripped over a strand of fettuccine,
Flew through a portal to a land quite weeny.
Pasta trees sprouted, with marinara rain,
I'd never seen such a glorious chain.

The meatball mountains loomed high and round,
While spaghetti rivers danced on the ground.
Forks were the traffic lights in this town,
Who's in charge? The ravioli crown!

Navigating Spaghetti Universes

Captain of pasta, I steer through the sauce,
Navigating noodles, at every great loss.
My spaceship's made of lasagna so grand,
We map out each twist with a firm noodle hand.

Black holes are just deep, meaty bowls,
Eating the cosmos is how we reach goals.
With every big bite, a star disappears,
As laughter erupts through the galaxy's cheers.

Culinary Tales from the Cosmos

In a galaxy far, where chefs wear big hats,
Pasta planets orbit like curious cats.
They twirl and they whirl in a cosmic embrace,
With each slurp, we savor the vastness of space.

Vermicelli comets soar over our heads,
As mozzarella moons light up our beds.
Let's feast on the stars, and twirl with delight,
In this kitchen of chaos, the universe bites!

Noodles of the Cosmos

In a pot of stars, the noodles whirl,
Saucy comets dance, giving a twirl.
Galaxies slurp their spaghetti delight,
While aliens munch on their pasta at night.

With each twist and turn, gravity bends,
Wormholes serve pesto; the fun never ends.
Twirl up the noodles, let the time fly,
Savor the flavors of this cosmic pie.

Twisted Tides of Space

In the pasta stream, the planets collide,
Fusilli asteroids take us for a ride.
Zany pasta shapes, the universe's flair,
Penne meteors zoom through the air.

Oodles of noodles weave tales of delight,
As galaxies giggle in the warmth of the night.
Tangled spaghetti in a cosmic embrace,
Laughing together in the fabric of space.

Pasta Dreams in a Black Hole

Diving through darkness, we find a delight,
Noodles in the void spin around in the night.
Saucy and slippery, they pull us within,
Pastas align like a dream in a spin.

With each incredible slurp, time goes askew,
Gravity laughs as it pulls us right through.
Softly entangled in a creamy embrace,
Pasta for dinner, in this infinite space.

The Tangled Threads of Time

Whisked by the whiskers of time and of fate,
Pasta loops round, making history great.
From fettuccine futures to elbow-shaped pasts,
The sauce of the cosmos forever lasts.

Noodles entwined, now what shall we do?
Serve up the laughter, add some giggle brew.
As time slips away, served al dente,
Let's feast on the fun wrapped in every entry.

Cosmic Slurps

In space, the pasta twirls and spins,
A noodle dance where chaos begins.
Galaxies might giggle, stars may snicker,
As sauces swirl like comets quicker.

Black holes take a slurp, oh what a sight,
Sucking up the spaghetti with delight.
Even aliens with forks start to cheer,
For cosmic meals served far and near.

Universes Entwined

Two pasta worlds collide with a splash,
Each noodle stretching, like a goofy sash.
Sauce pots jiggle, gravity's loose,
As forks are tangled, forming a truce.

With every twist, the cosmos roars,
While spaghetti hunters rush through the doors.
A universal dinner, far from dread,
Where pasta dreams are lovingly fed.

Tangled in the Singularity

A cosmic knot of glimmering strands,
Pasta intertwined like dance in bands.
Slippery noodles slide with glee,
Caught in a whirl of pure jubilee.

Warped by gravity, a hilarious plight,
As spaghetti swirls in the starry night.
The sauce spills over, laughter ensues,
In a universe where no one can lose.

Distortion on a Celestial Plate

On a plate of stars, a feast awaits,
Galactic meals served on fun-filled plates.
Gravity bends, making spaghetti swirl,
As we twirl and laugh in the cosmic whirl.

Sauce rips through fabric, it's quite absurd,
A pasta party where quirks are stirred.
So come join the fun in this tasty abyss,
Where every bite's a hilarious twist, oh bliss!

Gourmets of the Galactic Pit

In a cosmic kitchen, pots do whirl,
Spaghetti takes a dive, gives a twirl.
Alfredo sauce in zero-G,
Noodles dance like joyfully free!

Space chefs toss in garlic and flair,
While aliens float without a care.
With every bite, they howl and cheer,
Their soufflés taste of starry beer!

Italian Vortex of Life

Down the spiral of the pasta drain,
Tomato meteors fall like rain.
Fettuccine stars, so long and bright,
Twirl around in pure delight!

Each bite pulls us back, it's a fight,
To not drift off into savory night.
With every forkful, oh, what a ride!
It's pasta love, with no one to hide!

Entangled Threads of Love

In the cosmos of carbs, we weave,
A noodle heart that won't deceive.
Twisted together, so soft, so real,
Our pasta love, a glorious meal!

Mario grins from his kitchen throne,
Slinging strands through the cosmos alone.
Al dente hugs, with sauce so bold,
In the galaxy, our hearts unfold!

Pasta Constellations

Under starlit marinara skies,
Spaghetti shapes the universe's sighs.
Stars twirl like ravioli in a pan,
In this cosmic feast, we joyfully plan!

Saucy comets zoom with cheesy glows,
Orbits of pesto, heaven's prose.
Galactic diners with plates so wide,
Savoring the cosmos, oh, what a ride!

A Plate Full of Paradoxes

In a bowl of thoughts, noodles twist,
Sauce of time, impossible to resist.
Forks dive deep, thoughts intertwine,
Dining on chaos, oh how divine!

Gravity's game in this savory plight,
Slurping logic, day turns to night.
Forking the future, what shall we find?
A paradox served, carefully entwined.

Pasta Nebulae and Scalar Curries

In a cosmic pan, spices collide,
Pasta like planets, take a wild ride.
Curry so bright, it stretches the skies,
Saucy delights, to fill up our eyes.

Noodles like stars, twirling in flight,
Eclipsing our hunger, in culinary night.
A bowl filled with marvel, flavors galore,
Galaxies dance on a tastebud's floor.

Ethereal Loops of Delight

In spirals of fun, the noodles are free,
Twists of enjoyment, oh can't you see?
With laughter we twirl, in this gourmet race,
Each bite a loop, a delicious embrace.

Al dente dreams, of flavors unfurl,
Cascading in tangents, as taste buds whirl.
Ethereal delights, in every twine,
Who knew pasta could stretch space and time?

Time-Traveling Trattoria

Step in the door, where past meets the now,
Pasta from ages, take a savory bow.
Each forkful whispers secrets long lost,
In every delicious, transcendent toss.

Moments alight on the edge of a plate,
Stirring up futures as we contemplate.
From ancient Rome to the year twenty-three,
A trattoria's magic, oh what a spree!

Orbital Threads of Passion

In the dance of time, we twirl,
With noodles long and sauces swirl.
Galaxies made of fettuccine,
In the cosmic pot, it's quite the scene-y.

Gravity's pull, a tasty fight,
Alfredo dreams and marinara delight.
Twist and turn, like pasta on a fork,
Our hearts collide at the tasty cork.

Down the cosmic drain we slide,
With meatballs big, we take the ride.
Through black holes, sauce will flow,
In the universe of carbs, we glow.

A friendly galaxy, we embrace,
Where every meal's a warm embrace.
With laughter ringing through the dark,
Our friendship shines, a saucy spark.

The Charmed Spiral of Matter

In the depths of the cosmic pie,
Spaghetti planets do not lie.
With every loop, a twirl and twist,
You'll find laughter in the cosmic mist.

Pasta stars in the endless night,
Dancing with sauce, a charming sight.
Fusilli dreams, corkscrew fun,
We spin through galaxies, everyone.

The edge of taste, where flavors meet,
A charm of spirals, oh, what a treat!
With breadsticks as our telescopes wide,
We observe the universe's snickering tide.

From the sauce of life, we all emerge,
In this cosmic kitchen, we converge.
Sharing bites and joyful cheer,
In the spiral dance, we persevere.

A Feast at the Edge of the Unknown

Gather 'round the cosmic table,
Where pasta dreams are all quite stable.
A feast of stars on dishes bright,
With laughter served, 'til the morning light.

At the edge of the great abyss,
Lies pesto sky and cheese's kiss.
As we twirl our forks in glee,
The universe sings a pasta spree.

Galactic salads tossed with flair,
Across the void, we dine and share.
With jokes about black holes and space,
This cosmic meal finds its own place.

Eating noodles light-years long,
In this absurdity, we belong.
With each bite, our spirits soar,
In this feast, we crave for more.

The Great Pasta Expansion

Once upon a time in a cosmic bowl,
Noodles stretched beyond control.
With sauces thick and spices bold,
A hearty tale is there to be told.

The universe twirls in a cheesy spin,
As we create chaos with a grin.
Galactic grains on plates laid out,
With every bite, we laugh and shout!

Oh, the expanding realms of taste,
Even time can't make us waste.
As meatballs gravitate near our hearts,
This jesting journey truly starts.

With every noodle, a laughter binds,
In the great beyond, the fun unwinds.
So twirl this life with all your zest,
In the pasta cosmos, we are blessed.

Seasoned by Stars

Noodles dance in cosmic sauce,
Twinkling with a starlit gloss.
Galactic forks on the table spread,
Slurping comets, nothing's dead.

Gravity's the chef, oh what a feat,
Boiling black holes, life's gourmet treat.
With every bite, we spin and twirl,
In this pasta dream, the galaxies swirl.

Beyond the Event Horizon's Plate

Pasta enters, never comes back,
The sauce promises, but it's a trap!
In the kitchen of doom, we all scream,
Is that alfredo or a wibbly dream?

Gravity's pull, it shapes the dish,
Saucers colliding—oh what a wish!
Each slurp's a journey, so bizarre,
Beyond the plate, we reach for a star.

Taste of the Celestial Web

Webs of spaghetti, so divine,
Ghostly flavors make us pine.
Milky Way's sauce drizzled with care,
A cosmic meal we want to share.

Planets twirl in a bowl, oh what glee,
Eating stars is the key, you see!
Galactic spaghetti, twirling with grace,
In the universe's warm embrace.

Slurping the Void

In the void, we slurp with delight,
Pasta loops that dance in the night.
With a pinch of stardust, a sprinkle of fun,
Every bite's a victory, we've just begun.

Wormholes twist to the plate's suggestion,
Every noodle's a taste of celestial lesson.
Laughter flows as we twirl and dive,
In this funny banquet, we feel alive!

Al Dente in the Abyss

In a pot where noodles twirl and spin,
I ponder all the chaos that's within.
Gravity pulls on each pasta strand,
As forks reach out, a rather silly hand.

The sauce is bubbling, a creamy plight,
Noodles tangled up in a slippery fight.
A twist of fate, a whirl of glee,
Caught in this taste of absurdity.

Culinary Collapse

The chef in a frenzy, what a sight!
As spaghetti launches with all its might.
Meatballs roll like bowling pins in fun,
This kitchen chaos has just begun.

Pasta erupts in a stretchy flurry,
The timer dings, oh what a hurry!
A saucy splash, a noodle's high dive,
In this recipe gone wild, we thrive.

Luscious Limbs of Gravity

Pasta twists and bends in the air,
With blobs of sauce, I stop and stare.
A tangle of flavors, a wacky show,
As gravity laughs, "You think it'll go slow?"

Fettuccine flips like a dancer's dream,
In this noodle circus, we all must gleam.
With each plummet, I'm left in a daze,
Who thought cooking could lead to such praise?

A Spherical Dance of Pasta

Round and round the pasta rolls away,
Bouncing bright like a child at play.
In this edible globe, we twirl and glide,
As meatballs join in for a wild ride.

Ravioli join in for a jolly jig,
Dancing around to a playful gig.
With a twirl and a whirl, they spin so bold,
In this funny feast, together we fold.

The Infinite Bolognese

In the pot, the sauce does swirl,
Endless meatballs start to twirl.
Gravity pulls the pasta tight,
Dinner dreams in cosmic flight.

A bowl of chaos, twirling fast,
Time bends over, unsurpassed.
Sauce and noodles, a tangled dance,
Forks collide in wild romance.

Wait, is that a rogue noodles' flight?
One last bite, it's outta sight!
Kitchens caught in pasta's spree,
Who knew dinner could be so free?

A cosmic feast, mistaken blends,
Where every bite, the universe bends.
Pasta dreams and saucey schemes,
Laughs erupt in swirling streams.

Quantum Noodles on Cosmic Forks

In the kitchen, chaos reigns,
Noodles stretch in mystic chains.
Forks collide in playful jest,
Each slurp's a quantum quest.

Twirling threads of starlit fate,
Pasta cooked with love, not hate.
Light years pass with every bite,
Noodle leaps like stars at night.

A cosmic dance of flavors bold,
Spaghetti dreams too big to hold.
Sauce orbs twist in gravity's smile,
Taste the cosmos in a while.

Who needs stars when you've a plate,
Where meatballs spin and wobble straight?
This dinner's fun, a cosmic joke,
Nibble worlds one bite bespoke.

A Recipe for Starlight

Take a pinch of stardust bright,
Add it to the sauce, ignite!
Stirring in a galaxy's worth,
This meal's from the cosmic hearth.

Chop a comet, sauté it right,
Mix with laughter, pure delight.
Let the noodles twine and weave,
In every bite, the stars believe.

Simmer low on dreams of gold,
Hearty laughter, stories told.
A splash of whimsy on the side,
In this recipe, joy can't hide.

Garnish with a sprinkle of glee,
It's a dish you must agree.
Starlight soup, a cosmic show,
With every lick, the cosmos flows!

Temporal Twists of Pasta

In boiling water, minutes spin,
Noodles dance, let the fun begin.
Each twist and curl defies the clock,
A time traveler's pasta rock.

Long strands stretching through the years,
Sauce drips down like comets' tears.
Forks are time machines in disguise,
With every bite, the past complies.

Squiggly wiggly, tastes collide,
Dancing noodles, what's inside?
Each plate holds a history's tease,
In every forkful, giggles + cheese.

Oh, pasta time, you tricky sprite,
Make me laugh with every bite.
A meal that bends both time and space,
In future dreams, we'll find our place.

Diverging Flavors of Fate

In the cosmos, pasta dances wide,
With gravity pulling on every side.
Fettuccine dreams and spirals bright,
Twirling through the gaseous night.

A meatball rolling, oh what a chase,
Bouncing 'round the black hole's face.
Sauce spills out in a cosmic glow,
As noodles venture where few dare go.

The Pasta Paradox

In a pot of stars, noodles twirl,
A paradox in a cosmic whirl.
Al dente desires get stretched too tight,
Twisted dreams in the endless night.

Tomato sauce sloshes, physics defies,
While ravioli grins with pasta eyes.
Silly thoughts of flavors combined,
A feast of fate so whimsically designed.

Infinite Plates of Gravity

Infinite plates spin in space,
A banquet at a rapid pace.
Forks and spoons in a cosmic race,
Slurping noodles, oh what a place!

Giggles echo through time's embrace,
As gravity pulls with a cheeky grace.
Pasta comets streak the sky,
Every bite makes the stars fly high.

Twisted Fates in the Cosmic Kitchen

In a kitchen where stardust brews,
Fates get tangled with every chew.
Forks and knives wander off course,
Noodles giggle with a sly force.

Bubbling pots of perplexity,
Spinning tales of absurd complexity.
Lasagna layers stacked on high,
As comets whistle and spacetime sighs.

Universal Entanglements

In the cosmic kitchen, pasta swirls,
Stars twinkle like meatballs in curls.
A black hole's appetite never abates,
It slurps up galaxies, oh, what it takes!

Gravity's noodle pulls us all near,
While spacetime stretches, never shows fear.
In this vast pot, where things can combine,
I just hope my dinner isn't divine!

Sauce drips down the fabric of space,
As we laugh 'bout the galaxy's race.
Do we tango with quarks or just eat?
A universe served up on a plate so sweet!

As we chew on the mysteries, we find,
That silence of space can be rather unkind.
But amidst the chaos, in gluttonous chat,
We ponder the cosmos and giggle at that!

Cosmos on a Plate

A cosmic feast served on a fine dish,
With nebula soup that grants every wish.
The stars are the sprinkles, oh what a sight,
As we munch on the moons, shining so bright!

Black holes for dessert, oh what a treat,
They're full of surprises wrapped up neat.
With a bite of a comet, flavors collide,
In the galaxy's kitchen, there's nowhere to hide.

Supernova soufflé rises high,
While asteroid rolls make the taste buds cry.
Each nibble has laughter, each sip adds fun,
Celebrating the cosmos, one meal, just begun!

So grab your forks, it's time to explore,
The universe served, who could ask for more?
With cosmic delights at the table tonight,
Let's feast together till we take flight!

Celestial String Theory

In the energy strings, we dance and prance,
Twisted in orbits, we take a chance.
Harmonics of galaxies, a playful tune,
As we giggle under the light of the moon.

We pluck at the cosmos, each note a delight,
The universe hums, resonating bright.
Strings of spaghetti? Oh please, my dear,
With each tasty twist, we spin without fear!

Quantum sauce drizzled on math that's so sly,
Makes us twirl in circles, oh my, oh my!
With each slurp of time, a wink and a sigh,
We laugh as the cosmos flutters nearby.

In this kitchen of realms, let's stir and have fun,
Creating new flavors, we won't be outdone.
So grab your entangled utensils with glee,
Let's taste the universe, just you and me!

The Gravitational Embrace

Caught in the pull of a cosmic snare,
I'm tangled in stardust, take me if you dare.
Like pasta in sauce, we swirl and we twine,
In orbits of laughter that feel so divine.

The universe giggles as gravity hugs,
While planets keep dancing, giving us shrugs.
In this bizarre kitchen of fate and of fun,
We twirl in the orbits as one big bun!

With every embrace of a galactic star,
We chat about life, whether near or far.
Spinning like noodles, together we bend,
In our funny dimension, there's no end.

So come share a plate, with laughter so bold,
In the gravitational embrace, let's break the mold.
With a wink to the cosmos, and a nod to the night,
We'll savor the universe, oh what a delight!

The Melting of Cosmic Flavors

In space, pasta twists, a tangled spree,
Gravity's stretch makes it dance with glee.
Noodles long as comets streaking by,
Sauce from a distant star, oh my!

A meatball rolls, it wobbles around,
Floating free, in this cosmic playground.
Aliens munch while their ships collide,
Chewing on flavors from the great wide tide.

Sauce splatters on planets, rings of delight,
Fettuccine moons glow soft in the night.
Black holes fetch pasta into their grip,
Slurping spaghetti on a gravity trip!

Forks as rockets, in laughter we twirl,
In the universe's pot, we mix and swirl.
With each noodle bite, we'll giggle and cheer,
For dining in space brought the best of the year!

A Dance Beneath the Stars

Under the moon, the pasta does sway,
Twinkling stars join in a noodle ballet.
Twirling like spaghetti on a plate,
Cosmic dancers laugh, they celebrate!

Jupiter spins with a meatball in hand,
While Saturn's rings make a pasta band.
The stars can't help but shine down their light,
As noodles jiggle in the soft, starry night.

A cosmic macarena, what a sight to see,
With space-forks raised high, so joyfully!
Galactic giggles echo near and far,
While aliens salsa beneath every star.

We'll twirl through the void, pasta held tight,
In a swirl of flavors, what sheer delight!
So send out the call for a noodle parade,
In this universal dance, let's never fade!

Twirling the Cosmic Fork

In cosmic kitchens, pasta swirls,
Gravity's chef with noodles twirls.
Black hole sauce, a tasty blend,
Where flavors meet, and laughter bends.

Diners in orbit, what a sight!
Sipping star dust, oh what a bite!
Forks of light and spaghetti dreams,
Interstellar meals, or so it seems.

With every twist, a star is spun,
Sauce dripping light, oh, what fun!
Galactic feasts on plates so wide,
In dark matter's dance, we all glide.

So grab a fork and take a dive,
Into the cosmos, where tastes arrive.
Each noodle's length, a cosmic prank,
In the universe's endless tank.

Fusion of Flavors and Forces

Mixing flavors like cosmic rays,
In a pot where time delays.
Galactic broth, with stars to spice,
A taste that's cold as ice!

A sprinkle of helium and quirks,
Add a pinch of dark matter perks.
Pasta twinkling with supernova trails,
As laughter erupts, joy prevails.

Slurping galaxies in every bite,
Silly delight on a starry night.
With every noodle, a cosmic joke,
As we dine beneath the stardust cloak.

Fusion in the vast beyond,
With sauce and charm, we all respond.
The universe giggles in every slurp,
As we savor space with a happy burp.

Beyond the Event's Edge

They say the edge is where we meet,
Dark saucy tides for pasta treat.
Bending time with every taste,
Noodle waves we cannot waste.

Wormholes spill spaghetti flows,
In a cosmic mix, our laughter grows.
Gravity's pull, a jolly prank,
As we twirl our forks down the plank.

Sauce in a spiral, extra thick,
In crunchy asteroids, we take a lick.
Each bite a giggle, each slurp a cheer,
Past the edge, the fun is near!

Whirlpool pasta spins us 'round,
In the buffet of stars, joy is found.
So come on in and take a dive,
At the event's edge, we come alive.

Bowties and Black Holes

Bowties on stars, looking fine,
Laughing with every celestial line.
Dancing shadows in bowtie suits,
A gala in space, where fun just hoots!

Noodles flip like comets wild,
Each bowl a twinkle, an astral child.
A black hole's charm can't hold us back,
With silly laughs, we're on the track.

Light in a bowtie, so dapper and bright,
Zooming through cosmos, what a sight!
In sauce that bends like time itself,
We dine in style, forget the shelf.

Because every bite's a cosmic fling,
In our galaxy, let joy sing.
Bowties, black holes, a cosmic dance,
In this universe, we take a chance.

The Unraveling of Light

In a pinch, the stars can dance,
Wiggling free in cosmic pants.
When black holes spin with merry cheer,
They toss light beams just like beer.

Gravity's got quite the knack,
Pulling noodles from their pack.
Twisting, curling, with a grin,
A pasta party shall begin!

Catch a comet on a fork,
With sauce that'll make you gawk.
Stellar bites, what a delight,
As quarks twirl in the moonlight.

So let's laugh and have some fun,
In the soup where we all run.
When the universe finally sways,
It's all just cosmic gourmet days!

Cosmic Concoctions

Zipping through the galaxy's bowl,
Twirling galaxies take a stroll.
Mixing stardust with some spice,
Creating wonders, oh so nice!

In the pan where planets fry,
Sautéing dreams as comets fly.
A sprinkle of laughter, a dash of glee,
Is how we cook eternity!

As quasar sauce begins to thicken,
The universe's mouth starts to quicken.
Pasta swirling, colors flare,
Serenading the midnight air.

Galactic flavors, such a treat,
In this cosmic kitchen, life's a feat.
Grab a plate, enjoy the bite,
With every twirl, the stars ignite!

Celestial Carbs

Fluffy moons all dipped in cream,
Doughy comets form a beam.
Slicing galaxies like bread,
Nibble bites 'til you're well fed.

Stars are sprinkles in the night,
Flavorful bursts, oh what a sight!
Black holes serve as bowls of zest,
Time to chow down, no time to rest.

Pasta rings around the sun,
Spaghetti strands for everyone!
With each slurp, the cosmos hums,
As laughter dances on our tongues.

So twirl your fork and grab a star,
Galactic feasts are never far.
In our universe's vast embrace,
There are carbs scattered all over space!

The Gravity of Twirls

In the cosmic grip of fun,
Spinning planets just begun.
With every twirl, giggles thrive,
As gravity's whirligig comes alive.

Round and round the stars do play,
In a dance of night and day.
Each orbit, a chuckling tune,
Beneath a cosmic, giggling moon.

Noodle galaxies intertwine,
Making a pasta path divine.
In the whirl of the universe's laugh,
We find our silly, silly path.

So swirl with me, let's spin and glide,
In this cosmic kitchen, side by side.
Harvesting joy from every curl,
Life is one big twirling whirl!

The Fabric of Fettuccine

In kitchens where noodles dance and twirl,
Fettuccine dreams in a saucy swirl.
Gravity pulls, but joy holds tight,
As pasta spins under the warm moonlight.

With each bite, a chuckle escapes,
As forks twirl like rocket shapes.
Who knew carbs had such a draw?
In this delight, we find our flaw!

Twisted tales of cheesy lore,
In every dish, we crave for more.
Pasta hugs in a gooey embrace,
While laughter fills the empty space.

A spiral dance in the boiling pot,
Who knew dinner could be such a plot?
With every slurp, a giggle we share,
In this noodle galaxy, we float and care!

Gravitational Embrace

In the cosmic kitchen, chaos reigns,
As meatballs orbit, defying the chains.
Tomato sauce pools like stars in the night,
While garlic bread beams with pure delight.

Each plate a planet, spinning around,
With each optimistic flavor found.
The universe tastes a tad overdone,
Yet laughter flows like a trickling sun.

Pulling us close in a cheesy bind,
Stirring the cosmos, one pasta at a time.
When noodles collide, a giggle's in store,
In the dance of the spoons, we always want more!

Astronauts dream of resorting to carbs,
As they long for the warmth of a kitchen's charms.
Take your forks, explore this thrill,
In gravitational hugs, we always fulfill!

Pasta in a Black Hole

In the depths of the void, pasta gets lost,
Twirled into the dark, it's a heaping cost.
With sauce like a vortex, it pulls you near,
Until you're consumed by fettuccine fear.

Noodles spiral down, oh what a sight!
Singing songs of marinara delight.
"Help me!" the lasagna softly cries,
As ravioli flutters up to the skies.

The gravity's strong and the flavors galore,
As the garlic bread cries, "I want some more!"
With black holes that twist and twirl your fate,
You can't escape this delicious plate!

So twirl your fork in this timeless space,
Where laughter and pasta will always embrace.
As we dive into sauce, let euphoria reign,
With dinner as wild as a cosmic campaign!

Fluidity of the Stars

In cosmic cookbooks, the stars do collide,
With pasta in shapes that twinkle with pride.
Constellation noodles, all shapes and sizes,
Each bite leaves us laughing, oh what surprises!

The rigatoni forms a spiral dance,
As the moon takes a twirl, lost in the chance.
With creamy alfredo that flows like a stream,
Dinner tonight is a humorous dream.

Pasta stars shimmer, each sauce writes a tale,
A sprinkle of cheese gives a flavorful hail.
Galactic friends gather around the table,
While laughter erupts and we're all feeling stable.

So lift your forks like satellites bright,
In this comedic feast, we all delight.
With noodles like comets, we joyfully chase,
In the fluidity of stars, we find our place!

Entropy's Feast

In the kitchen chaos reigns supreme,
Pasta twists like a wobbly dream.
The tomato sauce is a cosmic swirl,
As noodles do the cha-cha whorl.

Sauce erupts like a supernova in flight,
Meatballs bounce with unbridled delight.
Forks and spoons like comets collide,
In this banquet where galaxies glide.

Gravity pulls at the cheese overhead,
As we twirl linguine, our bellies led.
With each silly slurp, laughter ensues,
In entropy's grip, we've nothing to lose.

So bring on the chaos, the tasty distress,
In this cosmic kitchen, we serve up success.
With giggles and gorging, we can't be beat,
In a universe where we dine and repeat.

Cosmic Currents of Amore

In a pot of water, love begins to boil,
As pasta pirouettes, it embraces the toil.
With butter flybys and basil twirls,
A cosmic romance cooked into swirls.

Sauces swirl like gravitational tides,
And each noodle dances as the flavor abides.
Garlic and laughter blend in the air,
As we stir our hearts, and we dance without care.

Gnocchi hugs in a warm, tender squeeze,
With a sprinkle of cheddar, we bring them to knees.
Two spoons share a moment, a well-fated fate,
In this pasta ballet, we relish the plate.

So let's twine our forks till the evening is done,
In this cosmic kitchen, we are astronomically fun.
With every bite taken, our tummies comply,
Cosmic currents of love make us flutter and fly.

Fractal Fettuccine Dances

Fettuccine loops in a wild fractal spree,
As tomato vines tango with glee.
Inspirations twirl, spiraling past,
Creating a pasta that's built to last.

Elbows twist like galaxies far,
While ravioli pirouettes like a twinkling star.
Each bite's an adventure in taste and design,
In this noodle ballet, we feel so divine.

Checkered tablecloths and wine glasses clink,
As we dive into sauce with a wink.
With each slurp and swirl, we indulge and prance,
In a cosmic soirée, we frolic and dance.

So raise a fork high, let the laughter unfold,
In a fractal feast, we'll forever be bold.
From noodles to stars, let good times advance,
In this universe, let's swirl and enhance!

Galaxy of Gluten

In the galaxy of gluten, we gather with cheer,
As pasta's gravity pulls everyone near.
Fried noodles and sauces collide with a grin,
In this universe hungry for joy to begin.

The universe boils in pots, bubbling bright,
As elbows and shells join in the fight.
Spaghetti takes wing like a comet on dive,
In this edible cosmos, we truly come alive.

Sauce splatters like stars on a canvas of white,
As we twirl our forks with all of our might.
With laughter as seasoning, we dive into fun,
In a galaxy where all flavors run.

So hoist up a plate, let your taste buds unite,
In this glutenous banquet, the future looks bright.
With each silly bite, let the good times unfold,
In this vast culinary space, all are bold.

Celestial Pasta Dreams

In the cosmos, noodles swirl,
Gravity's chef begins to twirl.
Sauce drips down from starry streams,
Dinner served in cosmic themes.

With each bite, the planets bend,
Eating shapes that twist and wend.
Marinara comets fly,
Pasta shapes make me wonder why!

Fettucine moons in orbit race,
While penne smiles in space's embrace.
Launch a fork through time's delight,
To taste the stars, oh what a sight!

Strung between celestial spheres,
Every mouthful calms my fears.
Noodle realms and galactic beams,
In pasta dreams, it seems it gleams.

Strings of Time and Space

A noodle here, a noodle there,
Time wraps 'round, I lose my hair.
Twisted strands of fate and fun,
Drawing joy 'til day is done.

Tangled up in cosmic whirls,
Spaghetti spins; the timeline swirls.
Each bite leads to a silly fate,
A banquet where the last is late.

Flying forks and flying sauce,
In this kitchen, I'm the boss.
Saucy black holes, oh so bold,
Of pasta futures, tales unfold.

Corkscrew paths of endless cheer,
Stretching flavors, bite them here!
In this dance of twirl and leap,
I laugh aloud while taste buds weep!

Twisted in the Abyss

In the void, where noodles twine,
A sauce ship sails through space divine.
With flavors lost, and laughter tossed,
Who knew pasta could be so embossed?

Fusilli frights in a blackened hole,
Spirals curling like a troll.
Gnocchi ghosts haunt every bite,
In the abyss, what a sight!

Pasta planets spin with cheer,
Making merry, bringing near.
Every al dente cheer and laugh,
In the universe, we share a half.

Oh, the joy of tangled strands,
Summoning giggles with our hands.
In this abyss, we dance and play,
Finding fun in a saucy way!

The Stretch of Existence

In the stretch of cosmic time,
Each noodle sings a silly rhyme.
With marinara stars above,
Life is tasty, everything to love.

Elastic dreams on an epic scale,
Twirled spaghetti making the tale.
Sauce from galaxies, no regret,
Laughter echoes, let's not fret!

Slinging sauce into the void,
Every swirl, a taste enjoyed.
With each forkful, we extend,
Space and laughter, they don't end.

As we noodle through the fun,
Each bite sparks a radiant sun.
In this stretch of joy and grace,
Existence tastes like a jolly race!

Noodles of Cosmic Whirl

In the kitchen, pasta takes flight,
Giggling as it dances in the night.
Sauce swirling like galaxies bright,
Forks poised to twirl with delight.

Al dente dreams and saucy delight,
Gravity pulling with all its might.
Noodles twist in a cosmic bite,
Sipping stars under the moonlight.

A colander caught in a black hole,
Pasta escaping, that's the goal.
Ravioli lost in a noodle roll,
Spaghetti sprawled in chaos whole.

So bring your forks, let's have some fun,
Cosmic comedy as we all run.
In the kitchen, our laughter spun,
With each twirl, a new joke begun.

Gravity's Lament

Oh, dear gravity, why are you cruel?
Pulling my pizza into the pool!
Pasta that dangles, a silly jewel,
Like spaghetti caught in a cosmic duel.

Fettuccine flies like a comet's tail,
Landing in sauce, we giggle and wail.
Our kitchen's a rocket on a tasty trail,
The noodles escape, and they leave a trail.

As I reach for a slurp, it escapes my grasp,
Caught in the vortex of a cosmic clasp.
Sipping the noodle, it's such a gasp,
In this kitchen adventure, we find our lisp.

So here's to the pasta that dances and swirls,
In the universe of food, the fun unfurls.
Gravity's a joker, as the laughter whirls,
In a feast of flavors, our joy twirls.

Tendrils of the Infinite

Tendrils of pasta reach for the sky,
Like starry strands that flip and fly.
Bubbly sauce laughs as we comply,
In this cosmic kitchen, we can't deny.

Over boiling thoughts like a vibrant sun,
Noodles warp and twist, oh what fun!
Each bite a burst, a joyful run,
Cosmic flavors, round we go, one by one.

As we slurp the noodles, giggles abound,
Shaping a black hole with flavors profound.
With each playful twirl, joy is found,
In the universe of pasta, we're spellbound.

So spin your fork in the cosmic dance,
In this funny world, we dare to prance.
Pasta and laughter, a merry romance,
Hold tight to your plate, give life a chance.

A Dance of Entropy

In the kitchen mix-up, a wild affair,
Noodles are twisting without a care.
Sauce splatters everywhere, oh beware,
Entropy laughing, a tangled snare.

Farfalle float like butterflies,
In this scenario, no one complies.
Pasta's a whirlpool where chaos flies,
With a fork in hand, we reach for the skies.

Rolling in laughter, meatballs collide,
Galactic flavors we cannot hide.
Each forkful's a journey, a delightful ride,
In this cosmic chaos, we take stride.

So gather your friends, the more the cheer,
In the dance of noodles, there's nothing to fear.
Cosmic giggles, oh so dear,
As we twirl and feast, let joy steer.

Flavors of the Cosmic Ballet

Twirl the stars in a cosmic bowl,
Pasta planets dance, what a goal!
Marinara comets drip and spin,
An interstellar feast to begin.

Fusilli galaxies swirl with glee,
Saucers of planets, oh can't you see?
Linguine orbits in spiral delight,
In this noodle world, everything's bright.

The chef of the cosmos throws in some spice,
Each star a meatball, oh so nice!
With a sprinkle of stardust on top,
Grab your forks, it's time for the hop!

Wobbling worlds in a big pot boil,
Chef Jupiter stirs while the moons toil,
Join the dance, give your taste buds a twirl,
In this kitchen of heavens, joy will unfurl.

The Space between the Noodles

In the cosmos where pasta's the theme,
Galactic strands pull, twirl, and dream.
Each black hole's a pot of boiling joy,
The universe cooks, oh what a ploy!

Spaghetti trails stretch from here to there,
Sauce-stained comets float through the air,
Gravity's noodles tug at your heart,
In this cosmic dish, we all play a part.

Alien chefs with their goofy grins,
Whisking up wonders as the fun begins,
Sifting stardust on a plate of stars,
Nibbling on Nebulas, oh, what are we, Mars?

Past the edges where flavors collide,
This is a banquet where all mysteries hide,
In the giggling void between every strand,
The taste of the cosmos at our command!

Consonance of Cosmic Culinary

In kitchens where black holes swirl and spin,
A cosmic chef wears a flour-dusted grin.
Planets roll in a pot of delight,
Cooking up laughter throughout the night.

Each noodle is a thread of joy unspooled,
Bubbles of stardust in sauce, they're ruled.
Twirling pasta in a galaxy bright,
A symphony of flavors, such a sight!

Gravitational pull on every plate,
Come taste the joy, it won't be late.
Tortellini moons dance in a cote,
Earth's golden garlic sings the note!

A scrumptious tune in the stellar stew,
Savor the galaxies, we'll eat 'til we're blue!
In this cosmic kitchen, we'll take our time,
As laughter and noodles perfectly rhyme.

Tryst of the Twisted Al Dente

When stars and noodles choose to romance,
They meet at twilight in a swirling dance.
Twisted fates on a cosmic plate,
Every bite lingers, it's simply great!

The pasta twinkles in the vacuum's embrace,
While black holes giggle, a chaotic place.
Lunar lasagna, a sight to behold,
Stories of flavors from ages of old.

Whimsical wonders in sauce now shine,
A celestial banquet with sparkling wine.
Time stretches as we savor the bite,
In the kitchen of stars, everything's right.

Join the parade of the spiraled delight,
With forks as our wands, we dance in the night.
In this love of noodles and stardust swirl,
Cosmic cuisine, let our laughter unfurl.

Cosmic Fusion Cuisine

Unraveling pasta in a dark void,
Evolving flavors from elsewhere, quite stoked.
Black holes bubbling, a cosmic stew,
Gravity's chef whips up a wild brew.

Forks twirl galaxies; taste buds collide,
Sippin' on stardust like it's a ride.
Celestial noodles, al dente delight,
Feasting with aliens, what a weird night!

Wormholes wriggle with a spicy zest,
Sauces so funky, they might just protest.
Galactic gatherings, a savory spree,
Whisking through nebulae, just you and me.

Chow down on quasars, oh what a feast,
Burp a big bang; our appetites increased.
Dining in starlight, the table's set wide,
A cosmic kitchen where laughter won't hide.

Strings of Celestial Spice

In the universe's pantry, a twist of fate,
We mix cosmic spices on this grand plate.
A sprinkle of stardust, a dash of black hole,
Cooking up chaos, it's how we roll.

Lasagna from planets, with layers galore,
While moons serve salad on a graviton floor.
Jupiters juggling with a side of delight,
Taste buds exploding, what a cosmic bite!

Gathering comets to sauté and fry,
Planets dance round, oh my, oh my!
With every bite, the cosmos ignites,
Savor the stars on these whimsical nights.

Celestial kitchens make time bend and swirl,
Taste the universe, give your senses a twirl.
Stringing together the flavors of space,
Lift up your forks; let's embrace this race!

Braided Threads of Existence

Pasta spirals like galaxies spin,
Crafted from stardust, where do we begin?
With every fork twirl, existence unfolds,
Tales of the cosmos, in flavors retold.

Braid of existence, a savory twist,
From black hole pies to a time-cooked mist.
Life forms merge in a swirl of delight,
Eating the whole universe, a grand appetite!

Sautéed supernovas on the cosmic grill,
Sippin' on energy drinks, catch the thrill.
Cosmic broth bubbles; watch it weave,
Threads of the universe, you won't believe!

In kitchens of the stars, laughter ignites,
Tasting the fabric, chewing on nights.
Each bite a journey, adventures unroll,
In this woven cosmos, we find our soul.

The Physics of Flavors

In the lab of laughter, we mix and blend,
A pinch of chaos, where flavor transcends.
Equations of taste in a bubbling pot,
Cooking up wonders in this funny plot.

Newton's laws tell us, keep food in line,
But who needs rules when the pasta's divine?
Gravity's pulling us closer to eat,
With each cheesy bite, we're feeling the heat.

Relativity's sauce, fast as light's beam,
A cosmic spread that's more than a dream.
Einstein would chuckle at planets on plates,
Wondering how we become such great mates.

Science collides; flavors take flight,
Bouncing around in this comic delight.
Join the mad table, let's have a cheer,
For physics of flavors, we're glad to be here!

The Cosmic Saucer

In the kitchen, pasta flies,
Twisting like stars in the skies.
Sauce spills over, oh what a mess!
Chasing noodles, we must confess.

Gravity's pull is strong, you see,
As I reach for that penne glee.
With meatballs dancing on the floor,
We're laughing 'til we can't take more.

A fork is a rocket, oh so grand,
Launching spaghetti across the land.
In this cosmic realm of taste and fun,
The meal's not over, it's just begun!

So twirl those noodles, give them a spin,
In a galaxy where we always win.
Pasta planets orbit in delight,
Eating until we see the light!

Noodle Dances at Light Speed

Under the stars, the noodles glide,
With marinara caught in the tide.
Linguine loops with a cheeky grin,
This pasta party is how we win!

Fettuccine feels an urge to race,
While ravioli strikes a bold pose space.
Lasagna layers competing in fun,
It's a noodle race, and we've just begun!

Wormholes of flavor twist and twirl,
As spaghetti swirls make our heads whirl.
Each bite a journey, gravity's tease,
As we savor this cosmic cheese!

At light speed, the forks take flight,
Pasta droplets glimmer, oh what a sight!
Laughter erupts with every strand,
In this galactic noodle wonderland.

Gravitational Grains of Ambrosia

In the pot, the grains take flight,
A charming dance, oh what a sight!
With each twirl, they defy the norm,
Creating chaos, a pasta storm.

Oodles of noodles waltz in the bowl,
With vibrant flavors that soothe the soul.
Each sprinkle of spice, a cosmic spark,
As we dive into the delicious arc.

Gelatin galaxies wobbly and round,
Falling into sauces, blissfully bound.
A spoonful of heaven, sweet and divine,
Gravitational tastes, a perfect design!

With laughter, we twirl this edible art,
In the universe of flavor, we take part.
So grab your fork, let's dine with glee,
In this amusing cosmic spree!

A Whirl of Spaghetti in the Abyss

In the void, spaghetti spins high,
With meaty comets whizzing by.
Saucy stars twinkle bright and bold,
In the abyss, tales of pasta are told.

Noodles twine like lost satellites,
Creating a symphony of favorite bites.
Each strand dances with gravity's grace,
In this infinite noodle embrace.

Meatball meteors flare with thrill,
As we slurp and giggle, what a skill!
Across the cosmos, flavors unite,
A whirl of laughter in the night.

So let's embrace this cosmic feast,
With every taste, our joy increased.
In this culinary void, we'll take a trip,
To the land of spaghetti, we'll happily skip!

Harmonies of the Event Horizon

In space where the noodles twist and turn,
Black holes serve pasta, oh how they burn!
Gravity grins with a playful tease,
While spaghetti dances in cosmic breezes.

Sauce drips off comets, a tangy delight,
Fettuccine comets flirt in the night.
Slurp those stars with a wink and a laugh,
As we noodle our way through the cosmic path.

Linguine loops in a glorious swirl,
The universe's recipe, what a great pearl!
Each bite a surprise, watch it crunch and pop,
In the kitchen of space, we just can't stop.

So raise up a fork, let us dig deep,
Into the cosmos where strange flavors leap.
With a dash of starlight and a sprinkle of cheer,
We'll feast on the universe, no need to fear!

Whispering Galaxies

Galaxies giggle in the light of the sun,
Whispers of pasta, oh what a pun!
Spaghetti twirls like a ballerina bright,
In the cosmic dance, it's a humorous sight.

In the Milky Way's pantry, stars are the spice,
Ame pasta comets, oh so very nice!
They slide and they glide with a flair so grand,
Making cosmic jokes that are perfectly planned.

Pasta floats freely where the black holes eat,
Grinning noodles in an endless retreat.
With a dash of humor and a splash of fun,
We'll laugh in the darkness 'til our journey is done.

So when you gaze up at the shimmering night,
Remember the laughter that dances in light.
In the kitchen of starlight, we all play a part,
With the universe's pasta, we fill up our heart!

Threads through the Void

Threads of spaghetti weave through the stars,
Knitting the cosmos with its twirls and bars.
Every strand holds a story, a laugh in each bite,
As we travel the void with appetite bright.

In the black holes' grip, the pasta does bend,
A great cosmic story that has no end.
With each playful loop, we twine and we fold,
Tales of the universe, ready to be told.

Carbon and cream, a stellar delight,
Sauces collide in the deep, starry night.
As we feast on these wonders, our spirits will soar,
In the threads of the void, we're hungry for more.

So lift up your bowl, let's share in the fun,
With gravity's laughter and a race to outrun.
In this galaxy kitchen, let's savor the ride,
With a cosmic buffet, let's enjoy the tide!

Pasta of the Cosmos

The cosmos serves up a pasta surprise,
Giggles and noodles dance in our eyes.
With each galactic swirl, we twirl a fork,
Feeding the nebula, while comets just gawk.

Lasagna layers of stars in the fold,
Jupiter's sauce is rather bold.
Planets boil in a celestial stew,
As aliens smile, "Come dine with us too!"

In the universe's pot, our dreams bubble up,
Filling our hearts with a radiant cup.
So grab on a meatball, let's laughter ignite,
In the pasta of cosmos, everything's bright.

So here's to the flavors of stellar delight,
With twinkling laughter that sparkles the night.
In the grand banquet hall of the universe wide,
We'll feast on forever, arms open wide!

Quantum Entanglement of Noodles

In the pot, they twist and swirl,
With gravitational pull, they twirl.
A noodle here, a noodle there,
Entangled dreams of pasta flair.

Spin me 'round in sauce so neat,
While basil waltzes to the beat.
Oh, what a dance! Oh, what a round!
In this kitchen, chaos found!

Spoon of fate, do not let go,
Al dente life, it steals the show.
In quantum strings, our dreams will meet,
With every slurp, we claim our seat!

So grab a fork, let's take a dive,
In noodle worlds, we come alive.
Each twisted loop, a cosmic jest,
In this pasta realm, we're truly blessed!

A Strain on the Fabric

A pasta strand, like a space-time seam,
Tugging at physics, what a dream!
With tomato sauce making a splash,
We're stretching fabric, oh what a clash!

Fork in hand, I'm in a race,
To capture noodles, oh what grace!
Each twist and turn, a comic scene,
Laughter bubbles, a joyful sheen.

In boiling water, the chaos brews,
Silly shapes we didn't choose.
Spaghetti clings like friends so tight,
In this hungry cosmos, it's quite a sight!

Each serving piled, a cosmic heap,
A strain on pasta, dreams to keep.
With every bite, we laugh and cheer,
In this goofy universe, dear!

Entropy's Pasta Plate

On entropy's plate, noodles collide,
With sauce so wild, they won't abide.
A twirling mess of flavor and fate,
In this banquet, we celebrate!

A dash of chaos, a sprinkle of fun,
In every bite, we come undone.
Oh, tangled noodles, a glorious sight,
In this kitchen, everything feels right!

With every forkful, systems break,
A comical twist, a cosmic shake.
As sauce flows free, the noodles play,
In a dance of entropy, hooray!

So grab your plates, let's share the mess,
Witness the pasta's wild excess.
In this delightful, tangled spree,
The universe laughs, just you and me!

The Stretched Symphony of Starlight

In cosmic kitchens, stars align,
With noodle strings, they intertwine.
A symphony of pasta bright,
In this starlit dish, pure delight!

A sprinkle of stardust on our plate,
As twinkling shapes begin to skate.
Each spaghetti strand a cosmic note,
In this melody, we happily float!

Bouncing balls of meatballs fly,
As flavor heroes soar the sky.
With every twirl, the laughter flows,
In this pasta realm, joy overflows!

So join the feast, let's sing and sway,
In the stretched symphony, we play.
With noodles cosmic, bright and fun,
Together we shine, two hearts as one!

Subatomic Strands of Desire

In tiny realms where quarks do dance,
Fleeting flirts in a physics romance.
Neutrons giggle, electrons spin,
In this chaotic love, who will win?

With bosons bumping, they steal a glance,
Atoms blush, they cannot enhance.
Hypothetical love, a particle tease,
Quantum affairs that aim to please.

In a collider's heart, hearts race with glee,
What's this attraction? Could it be me?
But alas, it's science that leads the pact,
In this universe, love's just abstract.

So here I stand, a proton alone,
Wishing for love in this atomic zone.
Yet here in the chaos, I find a spark,
For even in physics, love leaves its mark.

Twirls and Whirls of the Void

In the vacuum's arms, I take a twirl,
Sucked in by forces, I start to swirl.
Gravity giggles as I float around,
Playing leapfrog with the stars unbound.

Planets looking down, a cosmic show,
They cheer as I spin, putting on a glow.
Asteroids join in, they bump and glide,
It's a dance party in the cosmic tide.

With black holes lurking to steal my groove,
I dodge with flair, in this fancy move.
Warped space-time bends, tickles my feet,
As I cha-cha with the stardust beat.

But watch your step, dear galactic friend,
For in this waltz, there's no true end.
So let's dance wild, in this endless flight,
Forever spinning in the velvet night.

Cosmic Confections

In the bakery of stars, a treat awaits,
Galactic pastries on celestial plates.
With dough made of stardust, sugar from suns,
Let's bake a pie with a sprinkle of fun.

Nebulae rise like fluffy soufflés,
Swirling and twirling in colorful displays.
Frosted with comets, they're truly divine,
An interstellar dessert, oh how they shine!

Black hole brownies, rich and so dark,
One tiny bite leaves a luminous spark.
Quasar cupcakes, a big cosmic hit,
Filled with supernova, oh, take a bit!

So gather your forks, take a seat at the stars,
For the universe's treat is sweet to the bars.
With laughter and crumbs floating all around,
In this cosmic kitchen, joy can be found.

Melodies of the Event Horizon

At the edge of the abyss, a tune does play,
A symphony of time, in a cosmic ballet.
With rhythms of matter, and beats of light,
Music that echoes through the endless night.

Gravity sings a low, rumbling bass,
While photons dance in a shimmering race.
Twirling around, the galaxies hum,
As quasars join in, and pulsars thrum.

In the dark, bold notes steal the scene,
A harmony of forces, both wild and serene.
All set to the tempo of space's embrace,
Together we harmonize in this vast place.

So grab your cosmic mates, let's join the sound,
In the swirling whirlpool where no one's unbound.
With laughter and joy, we'll ride this wave,
In the melodies crafted by the brave.

www.ingramcontent.com/pod-product-compliance
Lightning Source LLC
Chambersburg PA
CBHW051651160426
43209CB00004B/873